Decision Making
and
Effective Management

Foundations for developing business

Era of Modern Management
HR. Sustainable Development

Ibrahim H. Hussney

Accredited Lecturer and Instructor

"Investing in building human beings is now at the top of the pyramid of states' concerns as the most important industry in this information age, as a result of nations realizing that their fate and future will always depend on the creativity of their citizens, and the extent of their challenge and response towards change always for the better....!!!!"

CONTENTS

Introduction...
Between decision-making and decision-taking

The study of how decision-making is considered one of the essential and pivotal topics for organizations, business institutions, and companies, as decision-making, is organically linked to both firstly the methods of thinking and secondly the nature of human behaviors. Of course, the professionalism of decision-making must be affected radically and linked to the stages of development of daily human life which prompted him to develop decision-making mechanisms as well as to adapt and interact with the developments that meet him in his life.

When we talk about organizations, business institutions, and various companies as an integrated administrative, production, or service system, this system has imposed on workers, especially senior management, the inevitability of dealing with the decision-making process based on specific calculations and strategies that ultimately seek to achieve the goals of those organizations and institutions, and companies, especially if it is related to a dispute between the operating units and each other, where decision-making comes to control the existing relationships in the internal environment of the organization, institution, or company, in a way that does not harm the course of the work wheel, or at the level of external relations that link those organizations, institutions, and companies in the external environment, in order to achieve the common interest of both sides.

History tells us about decision-making as an ancient phenomenon defined by ancient civilizations. The Greek historian "Thucydides" mentioned while recording his study of what was called the "Peloponnesian War" (404-431 BC) - noting a group of factors that were influencing the leaders of the Greek cities to prefer between decision-making towards choosing the track of war, the track of peace, the track of the alliance, or the track of building an empire, as it all depends on the circumstances that were facing them in that era of time.

Thucydides delved into his study, where his interest was not only focused on the strategic reasons for the Greeks in this period when choosing for decision-making, or the image of the environment in their minds but also touched on psychological factors such as fear, honor, and interest, those factors that were the motives for them to choose a decision that expresses their wishes or those of their communities. Thus, this effort can be considered within the framework of the study of decision-making and its causes as one of the forefronts of theoretical work in this context, and the Greek thought was dominated by the Platonic perspective, which indicates that the center of decision-making must remain in the hands of the rulers, and they have to carry out the task of implementing those decisions.

If we go beyond this era striking in the depth of history, we will find that through the various stages of time that have passed and until our time, those who rule the various countries of the world seek help in making all their decisions from the so-called advisors who are specialists and who enjoy wisdom and knowledge, especially the decision-making that relates to the country's foreign policy.

Going back to the period of the Islamic system of government, decision-making was entrusted to the people in authority, as they are the most knowledgeable and able to deal with developments, under the umbrella of the Shura system, which opens the way for developing a significant set of alternatives that help the decision-maker to deal easily and smoothly with all the problems been faces at the level of the internal or foreign policy of the state.

The development of human and living means of life, first as a result of the industrial revolution, and the development witnessed in that revolution in tools that reach the level of luxury in many cases, and secondly, as a result of the boom in communications and the ease of transportation between peoples and countries, and what this boom witnessed as well.

The development of those tools related to communication with its various technologies eventually promoted the shortening of time and distances between people under the umbrella of different structures for ways of life that were not known before.

From the aforementioned, and with the development of the course of the humanities in its various branches and its transition to what is called the stage of scientific materialism, this had the greatest impact towards abandoning the traditional approaches to decision-making, and the trend towards adopting curricula for renewed studies.

So, this development aim is to adapt to life's changes, especially about the overlapping of human variables, such as psychological, social, economic, political, and other factors. These matters require decision-makers to develop an integrated theoretical framework for understanding, interpreting, and making these decisions without ignoring these variables.

Accordingly, many scientific theories and approaches have been developed related to human behavioral studies, such as modeling and simulation, for example, which greatly benefited decision-makers, especially in terms of achieving the goal of its maker and its impact on its recipients.

In the end, it remains to be mentioned that decision-making in this modern era must be based on correct data and information about the variables it addresses, and the structures of the strategies upon which it is built, in order to achieve the desired goals and obtain the correct and required results from the implementation of this decision.

The decision-making process may seem to some to be a simple matter that can be resolved in a few minutes, but the truth indicates that this matter is fraught with difficulty and complications, especially if this decision is related to the fate of organizations, business institutions, and companies. Decision-making is not an abstract process, but rather a process that includes many effects of related variables.

Among the controls, determinants, and choices of alternatives in order to resolve matters, we will find that there is what is called **the most appropriate alternative**, and there is **the optimal alternative**, and each of them has a price and cost.

Also, the decision-making process must take into account the situation of the decision-maker, his accumulated experience, and other supporting factors, and also takes into account the interaction of the recipient of the decision, and decision-making process also should take into account the effects of the external and internal environment of organizations, and also the effects of the interfering environment between them.

We must differentiate between the concept of *decision-making* and the concept of *decision-taking*. The decision-making process is a process that passes through a number of stages, starting with identifying the topic or problem and taking note of all the details, then moving to the analysis stage, followed by the evaluation stage for this topic or problem, and then collecting information In order to make the decision by first proposing appropriate solutions, and working on evaluating them so that in the end the best one can be chosen among them.

The decision-taking process refers to the conclusion reached by the decision-maker / makers, after completing the collection of information and ideas about the topic or problem under discussion and finding a number of alternatives and solutions. As for the decision-taking process, it is the process in which the choice of the most appropriate solution, or the best out of a set of choices, is in the form of a decision made by a person or persons authorized to do so.

And on the occasion that we are talking about decision-making, I chose to present to you the five best titles from the books offered on the Amazon platform, which talk about this topic, and they are, in order, the first book entitled Decisive, which talks about how to make better choices in

Life and Work, where the authors discuss some of the common mistakes we make when making some decisions, to avoid these mistakes, the authors present a method that we can follow to make better decisions, so they suggest resorting to following the method called (WRAP), which refers to expanding your options, testing your assumptions based on reality, and making some distance before making your decision. And be prepared to accept your mistake.

The second book is titled, Thinking of Bets, where the philosophy of this book revolves around the saying, make smarter decisions when you do not have all the facts, and here the author points out that we often build the "correctness" of our decisions based on the outcome rather than our decision-making process, as well as our thinking of our decisions as "right or wrong".

The important thing is that we make the best decision based on what we have and what we know, and our good decision is not based on our feeling of winning it, but on the process that we used to make this decision, and the author of the book adds, that if we do this through our daily decisions that we make, then we will make better decisions not only as individuals but as groups as well and that this will make us welcome the interventions of others and accept disagreement.

The third book is entitled, (Smart Choices), which reflects the practical guide to making better decisions, and these choices revolve around the guessing mechanism, that is, the name of the thing or the topic reflects the possibility for you to make smart choices. The three authors of this book have established a method in order to obtain these smart choices called (PROACT - with a URL at the end), each letter of which indicates an action that contributes to selecting the smart choice, the first letter refers to working on the problem of the right decision, the second letter refers to setting goals, the third to creating innovative alternatives, the fourth to understanding the consequences and conflict with preferences, the fifth to clarifying doubts and thinking carefully about taking risks, and the sixth to considering related decisions.

The fourth book is entitled (Thinking, Fast, and Slow), by its author won the Nobel Prize in Economics. This book relates to the details of the work of the human mind, with its logical and innovative system, and an explanation of some of the errors that we are exposed to.

The fifth book is entitled the paradox towards choice, as this book reflects a basic hypothesis, indicating that we exist in a world saturated with more and more choices, and this matter causes us to harm rather than help, they are the mistakes that result from your decision-making, which you can't even know. When we have many options, it not only makes it more difficult to make an option, but it also makes the choice we make less satisfying.

Chapter one…
General meaning of the word decision and its modern concept

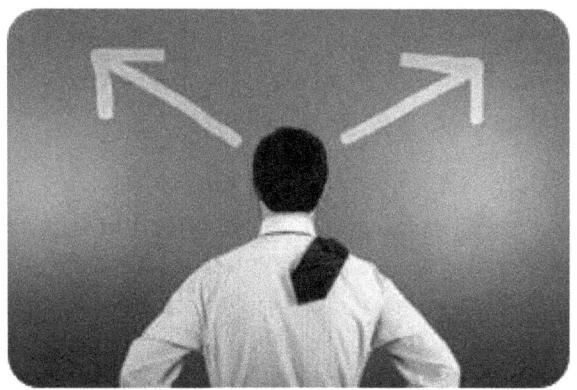

What does the word decision mean to you?

The issue of decision-making is considered one of the topics of great importance in the arena of science and modern knowledge, as this matter was the subject of great controversy among scholars, especially those with contact with social sciences, the management or political sciences, or those sciences related to human interactions, and the importance of decision-making stems from two main things. The first relates to academic matters, as this revolves around attempts to reach a general theory that will eventually be able to lay down interpretive and integrated foundations for understanding and studying the decision-making process. These decisions are of seriousness or importance as they express positions, goals, and strategies.

The reality of the situation informs us of the lack of access to a specific theory or any set whose foundations or rules can be agreed upon as a kind of guiding methodology for decision-making, as this comes as a result of the fact that social phenomena are always measured in relative terms and not in absolute terms, also, since it is in continuous movement and development, then attempts to combine comparative advantage and mobility may make the study of decision-making miss any of the general theories related to the study of decision-making strategies.

The thing which resulted in diversity and differences between specialized studies in this field, but rather the matter has reached a kind of contradiction in many cases, but despite that, many efforts have been made towards reaching the scientific concept of the decision itself, and the nature of decision-making according to the various topics that it deals with.

The general concept of the word decision indicates that it is a human act that reflects the final decision and the specific will of the decision-maker regarding what should and should not be done to reach a specific situation or a specific and final result, while *the modern concept* indicates that it is a path to do what the maker chooses as the most appropriate means available to him to achieve a goal, or it is a set of goals that he needs to achieve or to solve a problem or manage a crisis.

Sources of decision making

The decision-making process is based on two sources, the first is what is called **the decision-producing source**, which comes through combining thinking with reflection on the matter and making the necessary calculations, that is, it is based on awareness, study, and approach, and the second source is called **the source that produces actions**, which arises automatically based on the momentary suggestion of a person, which ultimately leads to the production of immediate actions.

Hence, we can define the decision as a path to do what its maker chooses as the most appropriate means available to him to accomplish a goal or set of goals that he wants to achieve or to solve a problem or manage a crisis, and some may see that the decision in its simplest case is a means that activates a response from the receiver performed by its maker, or the decision at complex levels may become a means of determining the parameters of a generally accepted response from the recipients where there was no response pre-existing.

Among other definitions of decision, Max Landsberg considered that a managerial decision is *"the implied process through which one person reaches to make a choice that influences the behavior of others in the organization towards their contribution to achieving its goals."*

The scientific concept of the decision-making process

The scientific concept of the decision-making process reflects the adoption of a set of constructive sequential steps in a scientific way to choose the most appropriate or optimal alternative to confront a specific situation, and the concept of decision-making does not mean only the adoption of the decision, but rather it is a very complex process in which other matters of multiple dimensions overlap, and therefore we can consider it as a method of rational selection among the available alternatives to achieve a specific goal.

Here we must stop at differentiating between decision-making and decision-taking and defining the scope of each of them because the concept of decision-making does not only mean decision-taking, but rather it is a very complex process in which other matters with multiple dimensions overlap, including what is primarily psychological, and perhaps political, or economic or social, and decision-making includes many other elements.

Among some opinions in this regard, we find that both Thompson and Tuden, in their talk about administrative systems, mentioned that, although the choice between alternatives seems ultimately to refer to decision-making, the concept of decision is not limited to the final choice for it, but rather it also refers to those activities that lead to that choice, and from here we must differentiate between the concepts of decision-making and decision-taking, as the latter represents an extended stage from the first, in the sense that decision-taking represents the last stage in the decision-making process.

Finally, we can point out that the decision-making process can be defined as a method of rational selection among the available alternatives to achieve a specific goal, and that this choice must depend on the following three tracks:

1- Decision-making must be done by following several successive steps that form a logical and innovative method toward reaching the most appropriate solution.

2- It must be trusted that for any situation, general problem, crisis, or risk there are alternative solutions that must be identified, analyzed, and compared based on specific rules or standards.

3- The method of discovering alternatives, defining selection rules, and choosing the optimal or most appropriate solution depends on a goal or set of goals that can be achieved, and also on the main criterion for measuring the effectiveness of the decision to be adopted.

Also, the decision-making process must revolve and be activated through a specific framework that includes six elements, namely, **the subject matter of the decision (case, problem, crisis, risks, etc.), the decision-maker, the strategy and purpose of the decision, the available alternatives, the rules for selecting alternatives, and the procedural process for selecting the optimal or most appropriate alternative.**

Structural tracks of the decision-making process

Decision-making must take place by following several successive steps that constitute a logical and innovative method toward reaching the most appropriate or optimal solution. These steps must include the inevitability of trusting that for any situation, general problem, crisis, or risk, there are alternative solutions that must be identified, analyzed, and compared based on the rules or specific metrics.

And that the method of discovering alternatives and determining the selection rules, and choosing the optimal or most appropriate solution, depends on a goal or set of goals that can be achieved, and also depends on the main criterion for measuring the effectiveness of the decision to be adopted.

In addition, the controls and determinants of the framework of the decision-making process must include the type and nature of the subject of the decision, the capabilities and readiness of the decision-maker, the strategy and purpose of this decision, the available alternatives, the rules of choice, and whether the choice will be the most appropriate or optimal.

Structural building of decision-making and its implementation environments

The structural building of decision-making is based on each of the methods of thinking used by the decision-maker and the decision-taker. It also depends on models of human interaction for the decision-maker and the decision-taker. It also takes into account the strategies and objectives required to be reached in the internal environment of the organization, business enterprise, or company, as well as both the external environment and the interfering environment between the two.

Factors affecting the decision-making process

Four factors affect the decision-making process, starting with the behavior of the decision-maker and the standards required of him, secondly, the reality of the issue and the facts and information it contains, thirdly the strategies and goals of the organization, business enterprise, or company, and fourthly the prevailing culture in the societal environment surrounding decision-making.

1- Decision maker behaviors and required standards

Behavioral standards for the decision maker play a major role in the birth of the decision that is characterized by appropriateness and balance and achieving the desired benefit from it. For this reason, the behavioral framework of the decision-maker has been included in three aspects:

The first aspect, which relates to the individual's subjective motives and their reasonableness, through which the individual's psychological behavior towards decision-making can be explained.

The second aspect, which is related to the psychological environment of the individual, is considered the main source that guides the person to choose the alternative that is closest to him in terms of being the most suitable among the alternatives in front of him and then comes the decision-making.

The third aspect is the standards related to the organization of decision-making and a course toward creating the self-environment for the decision-maker, through the following:

1- Determine the strategies and objectives envisaged in making this decision.

2- A period with the required information, data, and available alternatives to which he can resort.

3- Granting the necessary amount of authority, and defining the framework of responsibility assigned to him for decision-making.

4- Allowing him to practice a course towards decision-making through the appropriate tracks for him, whether administrative, technical, financial...etc., to gain experience through the existing organization of the intended decision-making.

2- The reality and what it contains of available facts and information

Is the value or ethical content, as some call it, sufficient to support decision-making?

Undoubtedly, the value content or the ethical content, as some call it, is not sufficient to support decision-making, instead, the content of reality must be taken into account, including facts that contribute towards differentiation in terms of alternatives or means that are weighted against choices or other means, according to the available information and data.

3- Strategies and goals of the organization

No one denies that any decision that is made and then adopted and then implemented must bear fruit and ultimately lead to achieving the goals and strategies of the organization, the business enterprise, the company, or even the society in which the decision is implemented. The goals and strategies of the organization or business enterprise or the company is the main track of guidance for all its operations, so the focus of attention towards decision-making will emphasize choosing the most appropriate alternatives or means that will achieve the goals of the organization, institution, or company on the tactical or strategic level.

4- The prevailing culture in the societal environment surrounding decision-making

The societal and cognitive culture surrounding decision-making, and in particular the pattern of prevailing and inherited values and traditions, is considered one of the important matters related to the decision-making process. Therefore, the social and cultural specifics of this society must be taken into account when making and taking decisions.

Chapter two ...
Classifying and categorizing the types of decisions that can be made

The types of decisions are categorized and classified according to their topics, or according to their nature criteria, or according to their importance, or according to the degree of their certainty, or according to the possibility of rescheduling them, or according to the required degree of change.

Classifying decisions according to their topics

They are decisions related to specific arrangements, such as agendas and work schedules, or decisions that work to identify problems and crises and set priorities for their consideration, or decisions that relate to specific procedures, such as those that adopt certain methods to provide solutions to problems and crises, or decisions that are characterized by cases of privatization, such as those that it refers to determining who implements what, when, where and how, or decisions related to evaluation, through which the achieved performance or achievement rates are measured and compared to the target, hoped or expected.

Classifying decisions according to the criteria of their nature

The nature of these decisions is controlled by some specific criteria that relate to their maker, and they are classified into two types, **delegating to the following levels**, and the second type is what is called **personal decisions**, and this type is concerned with decision-making that comes closest to the person who made it, his appreciation and self-values, and in this case, it is not possible to resort to adopting the delegation in it to the following levels.

Classifying decisions according to their importance

The importance of classifying these decisions for organizations, business institutions, and companies is controlled by three specific elements, namely **the strategic component, the tactical component, and the operational component.**

Frameworks for the strategic component of the decision

Strategic decisions are the decisions that concern the entity of the organization, business institution, or company and its relationship with the surrounding environment, which has great effects and dimensions on them, and their mutual relations with this environment, such as its general objectives, competitive situation, strategies, market options ... etc.

The features and advantages of strategic decisions are summarized towards targeting the exploitation of opportunities and avoiding risks, and these decisions are characterized by relative stability and are characterized by their long terms, as they consume large resources and a huge volume of information, and are resorted in the event of the availability of severe risks and cases of uncertainty, and these decisions are also characterized by a high degree of uncertainty centralization, as it is made by the top of the hierarchy of the organization, institution or company, i.e. by the higher management.

Frameworks for the tactical component of the decision

Tactical decisions are the decisions related to the preparation of plans and budgets and the use of financial, human, and material resources of the organization, business institution, or company to implement strategic decisions, such as allocating resources and deciding budgets, dividing tasks and functions, determining the paths of relations between workers, distributing powers, organizing work ... etc.

The features and advantages of tactical decisions are that they are characterized by change and medium deadlines. They are related to empowering strengths and addressing weaknesses. They deal with conditions of risk and relative certainty. They are made by middle administrations under the umbrella of relative decentralization and with a mandate from the authority.

Frameworks for the operational element of the decision

Operational decisions are most often related to the operational processes of the daily work wheel, and take the form of procedures and work rules related to individual jobs or work centers, such as forming teams and work programs, scheduling production, quality control, preparing orders, controlling inventory .... etc.

The features and advantages of operational decisions are summarized in that they are made based on previous experiences and are made immediately, and they do not require further effort, research, or creativity by their makers, and these decisions are characterized by short-term deadlines, as they always become related to the routine work method, and they are permanently repeated.

Examples of some decisions in terms of scope, purpose and importance

Field of decision making	Goal of decision making	Decision type
Organization's design	Organize operations	Tactical decision
Industrial methods	Manufacturing products	Strategic decision
Status	Place of manufacturing	Strategic decision
Maintenance	Scheduling maintenance programs	Operational decision
Structure	Structure of organizing works	Tactical decision
Job or occupation design	Best tool for design	Operational decision
Resort to technology	Best level of production	Strategic decision
Services	Services quality	Strategic decision
Teamwork	Numbers of workers and level of skills	Tactical decision
Annual inventory	What for organization and what against it	Operational decision

Chapter three …
Classifying decisions according to the degree of certainty of their results

Decisions are classified according to the degree of certainty of their results into *decisions with confirmed results*, which are the information and data on which decision-making is based that are available, accurate and complete, and the expected results of this decision are guaranteed and confirmed.

And *decisions with uncertain results*, which include missing or incomplete information and data, and then results of decision-making become uncertain, and therefore decisions are made within a framework of risk between the possibility of obtaining the desired results or not obtaining them, and this type of decisions can be scheduled in the framework more appropriate than the possibilities, which depends mainly on the meaning and quality of information and data available on the subject of the decision.

Decision-making can be classified based on the meaning and quality of information and data available on the subject of the decision, and in this regard, we can distribute these decisions on four aspects, for example, there is *the economic aspect* through which the available options are evaluated and the best decision-making is made, and there are **mathematical equations**, i.e. the use of mathematical functions, such as the utility function, and **statistical concepts** that are considered one of the applications of probability theory, and finally **consumer behavior** and the degree of his love for risk and its impact on the behavior of the decision maker.

Describe the degree of certainty of decision-making according to its importance

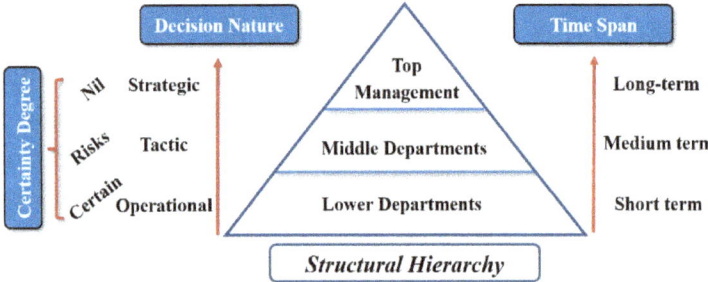

The description and measurement of the degree of certainty of decision-making according to its importance, and depends on two main factors related to the level that decides the organization, business institution, or company, **these two factors are both the period and the nature of the decision that is made**. Often the lower departments in the organization work on making decisions of an operational nature related to the daily work cycle, and these decisions are short-term, and the degree of certainty is confirmed.

While the middle management in the organization often makes decisions of a tactical nature, issued to develop, improve, or conduct business, which is of medium-term, and may be characterized by risk, and therefore the degree of certainty of these decisions seems to be medium.

As for the decisions that are made by the higher management of the organization, they are often related to the strategies of the organization, business enterprise, or company, and therefore they are decisions of a long-term strategic nature, and they may be exposed to great risks, and therefore the degree of certainty related to these decisions is considered low.

Classifying decisions according to the possibility of rescheduling them

Also, the decisions that are made in organizations, business institutions, and companies are classified *into decisions that can be rescheduled and decisions that cannot be rescheduled.* The decisions that can be rescheduled are those routine and recurring decisions that organizations, business institutions, and companies resort to, and they can be rescheduled according to administrative, financial, or technical procedures.

As for the decisions that cannot be rescheduled, they are those whose making requires the availability of special, specific, distinctive, or unique cases, such as decisions related to solving a problem or managing a crisis that occurs for the first time, and there is no prior and specific pattern or procedures known to solve it. This type of decision cannot be scheduled because problems or crises are characterized by the fact that their topics are not similar or coherent, which requires considering each case separately according to the circumstances and nature of its occurrence.

Comparing criteria between scheduled and unscheduled decisions

Comparing criteria	Scheduled decisions	Non-Scheduled decisions
Nature of the problem	Known, routine or frequent	Unknown and not frequent
Define alternatives	Available and known	It has kind of difficult
Decision making circumstances	Verification of results is available	Certainty is relative and risk available
Decision making procedures	Specified and known in advance	Unspecified and previously known
Supporting tools	Quantitative methods of analysis and advanced computer programs	Experience, intuition and advanced computer programs

Classifying decisions according to the required degree of change

The degree of change required is related to both the degree of influence of the decision and the nature of the situation. The degree of change comes either to solve a problem, manage a crisis, or avoid exposing the organization, business enterprise, or company to risks that threaten its business or entity or to bring about change to develop it and uphold its interest.

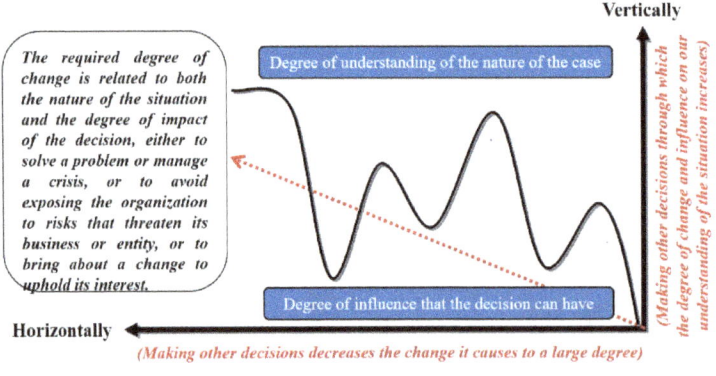

The required degree of change is related to both the nature of the situation and the degree of impact of the decision, either to solve a problem or manage a crisis, or to avoid exposing the organization to risks that threaten its business or entity, or to bring about a change to uphold its interest.

Degree of understanding of the nature of the case

Degree of influence that the decision can have

Vertically

(Making other decisions through which the degree of change and influence on our understanding of the situation increases)

Horizontally

(Making other decisions decreases the change it causes to a large degree)

From this illustration, we can discover that the degree of change required from decision-making depends on both the degree of understanding the nature of the situation that is the subject of the decision, and the degree of impact that the decision can have, which seems to fluctuate between ups and downs, as evidenced by the curve in the illustration, but it mostly takes an upward path, as the red arrow points.

The horizontal axis refers to other decision-making that decreases the change it causes to a large degree, while the vertical axis refers to other decision-making through which the degree of change and the impact on our understanding of the situation increases.

The importance of departmental participation in decision-making and teamwork

The factors that confirm the feasibility of the participation of various departments in organizations, business institutions, and companies towards decision-making are summed up in the exponential growth of the structures and entities of those organizations, business institutions, and companies, and their expansion, and the limited capabilities and abilities of the human mind of the individual, regardless of his knowledge and experience, also, his inability to understand all the circumstances and variables that accompany decision-making, and not to deny the importance of brainstorming and consultation at the level of all departments, especially the senior and leadership departments, embodies the expansion of the base of participation towards decision-making.

Expanding the scope of participation in decision-making will certainly lead to enriching these decisions, increasing their strength and solidity, and working to bridge the gaps from which the causes that may generate conflicts in the future may be exhausted, because these decisions will inevitably be greatly affected by various information and experiences, in addition to that all the procedures that were resorted to in making these decisions will become more appropriate to the requirements of the situation with which the participants in its industry interact.

In addition, each participant will become more interested in the situation as long as those approved decisions and procedures feel affected by him, which will give him more experience that raises both his competence and maturity towards participating in making other decisions in the future.

Participation of middle and lower department in decision-making	*Responsibility for the results of decision-making*
Absolutely no sharing	**Top Management**
Side participation in simple proposals	**Top Management**
Relative participation with suggestions on important topics	**Top Management**
Essential participation in consulting for important decision-making	**Relative responsibility for all departments**
Full participation for decision-making	**Responsibility for all participating departments**

From this table, we can learn about the gradation of participation from the different management levels towards decision-making in organizations, business institutions, and companies, and also identify the extent of this participation, and the degree of responsibility placed on the shoulders of the participants towards making this decision.

Max Landsberg comments on this matter by stating, *"While one person may be referred to as a decision-maker on behalf of the organization, it can easily be seen that others have contributed towards identifying problems, identifying and evaluating alternatives, and also reaching for the final choice, where the elements of the decision made through formal and informal channels of communication can be traced back to many people, accordingly, it must be considered that the decision-making process in organizations of itself, means a joint effort of more than one individual and is not in any way an individual effort for a specific person, regardless of his position in the administrative structure of the organization, even if the decision in its final form was issued by this individual."*

Considerations required to make a successful decision

The considerations required for successful decision-making include working on calculating and estimating the time available for decision-making, estimating the economic factor towards the cost of decision-making, the importance of maintaining the confidentiality of decisions that are made, and the importance of preserving job hierarchy distances within organizations.

Calculate available time according to the situation

The time available to senior and leadership management in organizations, to make certain decisions may be short or limited, as in the case of making decisions of an urgent nature. There is also the possibility that this participation may lead at the same time to the disruption of some other goals that may be more important, and therefore the decision-making senior management must resort to trade-offs and urgently weigh the feasibility of participation or not in decision-making.

In the case of non-urgent decisions, in this case, lower administration can participate with higher administration in making this type of decision, as this participation can take place either in a secondary, relative, basic, or complete way.

The economic cost of decision making

There is no doubt that participation in decision-making within organizations becomes an economically costly process when calculating the factors of time, effort, and the necessary preparation for it, especially in the case of resorting to the participation of external support or consulting, for this, senior management must take into account that the cost is not high so as not to cover the value of the advantages that result from participating in decision-making.

The requirement to maintain confidentiality of decisions

Every organization has its secrets that, of course, do not wish to be known or disclosed to competitors for their business, whether those businesses take the form of products or services, and therefore in such cases, never allowed to participate in middle administrations or the minimum or external assistance and advice towards making and taking decisions that may lead to the leakage of relevant information, which may benefit competitors and harm the organization.

The requirement to maintain job gradient distances

It should always be understood and known by all parties involved in decision-making, that such participation does not allow them to transgress the distance and functional responsibility specified in the regulations and laws regulating the work of organizations, in the sense that participation in decision-making does not become a trap to entrap middle administrations in errors that affect them or their future career in the organization, and on the other hand, such participation should not be at the expense of the authority of senior management and their position within the organization.

Chapter four ...
Theoretical approaches to decision making

Based on the theoretical research case, three entrances can be counted and resorted to for decision-making, and each of these entrances has its features and advantages. ***These entrances are the rational approach, the administrative approach, and the customary approach.***

The rational approach looks at the decision-making process and is based on an economic basis characterized by rationality, in which goals occupy the forefront, and considers several alternatives that help achieve those goals, and through this approach, the results of each of these alternatives (choices) are presented. And its repercussions, and from here comes the calculation of the gain or loss resulting from the adoption of each alternative, or a specific policy to the exclusion of others.

This model of theoretical approaches is used when studying several administrative decisions as well as in analyzing political decisions, as this approach provides a logical means to study each decision based on its data, alternatives, the easiest ways to implement it, and how to maximize such benefits.

However, the weakness of this approach is that it assumes that other non-objective factors do not influence decision-making, such as individuals' convictions and self-perceptions, their awareness of the available information, or their understanding of the nature of the problem or crisis facing them, and thus their ability to choose certain decisions or alternatives and neglecting others.

The administrative approach aims to study the critical and non-critical decisions from a purely administrative perspective, and it believes that any decision that is made comes as a result of a long process of deliberation between different groups, where each one of them represents a specific administration or body that seeks to be entrusted with decision-making.

For example, the financial manager represents his department and seeks to make a decisive financial decision that is applied and approved by the organization, as a whole, and seeks to entrust his management with the task of implementing this decision, which may result in competition between the various other departments regarding which one it can make and implement such critical decisions, at the lowest costs, to reach a radical solution to the problem or crisis in the shortest possible time.

In such cases, the decision that was made is not characterized by a purely rational nature, as we indicated earlier, but rather its birth came as a result of lengthy negotiations between the concerned departments and those entrusted with discussing issues about the organization such as human resources, production, marketing and sales departments.... etc.

In this case, the senior management represented by the Board of Directors may seek to work towards reconciling the requirements of each department involved in decision-making, and as a result, the decisions to be reached may not become decisive decisions, but decision-makers often tend to this case to postpone or postpone the solution of the related problem.

Here, we should differentiate between the meaning of the critical decision-making process and those non-critical decisions. In the case of critical decisions, the top management has the upper hand and domination towards making this decision, either by itself or with the relative participation of middle and lower administrations, according to the importance of the decision and the available information related to its making, such as strategic and tactical decisions, and as we mentioned above, non-critical decisions such as operational decisions, are left to the concerned departments and are made under the supervision and follow-up of the top management.

As for the customary approach, it is concerned with the belief that characterizes the individual decision-maker, that is, what he believes in, and the extent of his ability to perceive and absorb the information and data available to him, as well as the extent of his appreciation for the incentives and environmental variables surrounding him. Multiple psychological studies have proven that the convictions and ideology of the decision-maker allow him to accept some information, and also to perceive environmental factors that are consistent with what he believes in, and reject information or factors that are not consistent with what he believes.

Also, the ability of the groups surrounding the decision-maker, including consultants and other participants, to analyze the causes of the subject under discussion, or the crisis related to decision-making in a purely logical manner, will be directly affected by the belief pattern of the decision-maker.

Therefore, such a pattern must prevent the decision-maker from seeing all parts of the picture, and will also lead to preventing his subordinates and advisors directly from giving the necessary advice for making crucial decisions for the organization. In the end, we can say that this approach tends to try the analysis of the cognitive and perceptual structures of the decision-maker.

Different schools of decision making

The concept of the decision-making process has gone through four school types of thought during its development, each of which has its origin, methodology, and style of decision-making. The beginning was with what we can call **the classical school, then appear the school of human relations, followed by the quantitative school, and finally the behavioral school**.

Rules and Fundamentals of the Classical School «Mechanical Model»

It is the school based on three theories, supported by the administrative thought of organizations and institutions, and these three theories are **the scientific management theory of Frederick W. Taylor, the theory of basics of management by Henry Fayol, and the theory of bureaucracy of Max Weber**.

It is noticeable that these theories included different intellectual currents, but were similar in their final goals towards decision-making, and these intellectual currents appeared during close periods under the umbrella of similar economic and social conditions, and also under the dominance of the pattern of rationality and the interpretation of human behavior that was distinguished by rigid mentality. This school was distinguished by the following characteristics:

• *Mechanism:* It is considered the human element as a machine that should adapt to the work or the job. Therefore, the classical school of this approach was described as the mechanical model.

• *Rationalism:* It is considered that the rational individual works to increase productivity to the maximum extent possible, as this is the best way to reach productive sufficiency.

• *Idealism:* The theories of the classical school were based on what must be the case within the organization to be ideal.

• *Formalities:* Work to establish formalities to regulate the relations between individuals in organizations and their different organizational levels.

• *Knowledge:* Full knowledge of all variables that may affect the decision is required.

In general, the classical school neglected the decision-making process and did not give it sufficient attention, as it assumed that the actions of the decision-maker are rational actions through which he seeks to achieve the objectives of the organization at the lowest possible costs.

The classical school also adopted the concept of a closed system towards decision-making, because it did not take into account only a limited set of environmental factors, especially the relationship between the results of the possible alternatives (options) to solve the problem or manage the crisis, and the benefit determined by the decision-maker.

Rules, basics and disadvantages of the school of human relations

Given the factors neglected by the classical school towards decision-making, and the resulting shortcomings towards achieving the goals of the decision, the school of human relations came to address the criticisms that were leveled at the classical school, where it used many scientific approaches, such as sociology, psychology ... etc., where focused through the study of these sciences on the human aspects of the individual during the performance of his work, and as a result of this, the attention of the theory of this school dealt on the following aspects:

• Focus on leadership and supervision style within the organization.

• Facilitate communication and develop the informal role of the organization toward raising efficiency.

• Maximizing the existing personal relationships between individuals in the work environment of the organization.

This school raised its motto (supervision, leadership, and democracy), and adopted from that a method for making decisions, especially when involving workers in making these decisions. Otherwise, it neglected, in general, decision-making, as happened in the classical school.

Rules, basics and disadvantages of the quantitative school

The quantitative school relied on quantitative analysis methods, which were widely used in various areas of management, such as information systems, operations management, and systems analysis. Those who belong to this school see management as a logical process that can be expressed in the form of symbols and mathematical relationships, this is what is called **the model term**, and adopting the model method or the slogan *"management is a model"*, this has led to great successes in solving many problems and crisis management.

The quantitative school has contributed a lot to the path of decision-making, through its use of quantitative methods or what is called operations research, and it has also contributed to helping senior management in organizations when making decisions, as it is one of the important tools that can address problems and managing complex and compound crises, by following a logical, sequential path that includes the following elements:

• Work on defining the problem and formulating it tangibly and logically.

• Work on building a (quantitative) mathematical model that expresses the problem.

• Work to extract the most appropriate or optimal solution to the problem.

• Work on evaluating the chosen solution and then implementing it.

One of the most important features of the curriculum of this school is working on defining the problem and formulating it tangibly and logically, by building a mathematical (quantitative) model that expresses the problem and working to extract the most appropriate or optimal solution to the problem, as well as working to evaluate the chosen solution and then implement it. What was wrong with the methodology of this school is the difference in the logic of choosing the optimal or most appropriate solution.

Rules and fundamentals of behavioral school

The behaviorist school was established to correct the criticisms leveled at the previous schools, as it did not rely on the idea of the classical school that upheld the economic principle, nor did it adopt the idea of the school of human relations that upholds the value of societal ties.

What is credited to this school is that it provided a theoretical framework that helps in decision-making, as it believed that the administrative decision is the focus and basis of the administrative process, and it focused on studying the human behavior of the individual and the group working in the organization and it also added new concepts in the field of management, such as the principle of cooperation, informal organization, and the impact of incentives on workers...etc.

This school relied on four rules for decision making, namely ***the behavioral approach to the decision maker, decision hypotheses, decision making, and finally decision evaluation.***

The behavioral approach to the decision maker

The idea of the behavioral approach depends on the fact that the human being is the main axis in the production process through which he can lead it to the stage of sufficiency, and therefore this approach focused on the behavioral aspects of the administrative decision-maker and the psychological and social dimensions he is exposed to, bypassing at the same time the technical and environmental aspects of the productive process, and despite this, the behavioral school considered that organizations and institutions are an open system that is affected by the factors of the external environment, as well as the factors of the internal environment, as this school distinguished between the different types of rationalism.

The behaviorist approach has elevated personal rationality, unlike the classical school, which has elevated objective rationality, and the behavioral school has discovered shortcomings towards the concept of objective rationality and the economic criterion when making decisions, and between the decision-maker himself who cannot reach optimal or appropriate solutions to the relevant problem or crisis, maybe due to some reasons:

• The decision-maker faces many internal and external factors that he cannot control.

• The optimal or most appropriate alternative that is currently available may not be available tomorrow.

• That the solution alternatives available to the decision-maker may not be clear or known, and therefore the choice of one of these alternatives will ultimately depend on his ability and potential to study each of them and analyze their results.

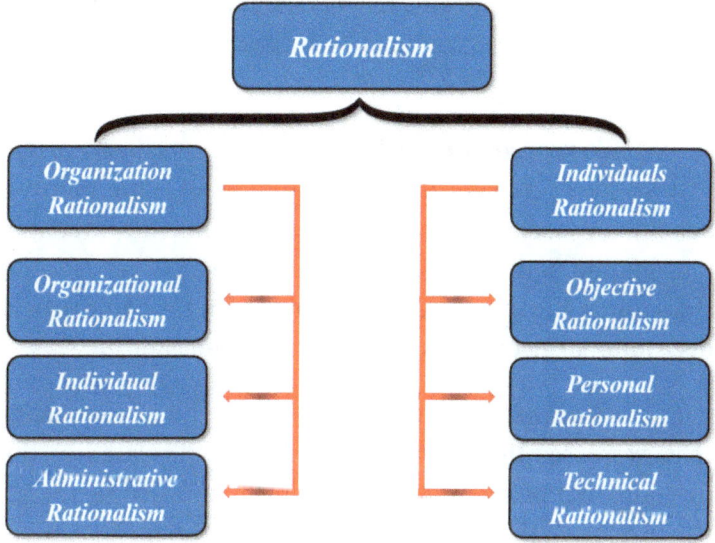

To avoid these obstacles, Herbert A. Simon suggested adding a qualitative criterion to the concept of rationality when using it, which gave it a kind of simplicity and realism, by classifying rationality into rationality that stems from the behavior of individuals, and rationality that stems from the behavior of the organization, and he divided the different forms of rationalism into six types, as shown in the previous illustration.

Types of rationalism and its characteristics according to the concept of Herbert Alexander Simon

• *Objective Rationalism*, which is the behavior that stems from the objective reality towards working to maximize the benefit, as that benefit is maximized in certain cases, and based on the availability of sufficient information and data about the alternatives (solutions) available to choose between them, with knowledge of the results of each of them.

• *Personal Rationalism*, which reflects the behavior that seeks to maximize the possibilities of obtaining the benefit in certain cases, by relying on the available information and data after taking into account all the constraints and other factors that may limit the ability of the decision-maker towards differentiation and choice.

• *Technical Rationalism*, is the type of rationality that expresses the management's behavior related to the development of scientific and technical knowledge and its use to achieve the objectives of the organization.

• *Organizational Rationalism*, this rationality expresses the behavior of the decision-maker related to achieving the objectives of the organization.

• *Individual Rationalism*, which reflects the decision-maker's behavior related to achieving their personal goals.

• *Administrative Rationalism*, is the rationality that expresses behavior that depends on resorting to the best administrative methods that lead to directing the work of individuals in the organization.

Despite reaching, through this classification, the separation and distinction of the types of rationalism, the adoption of the principle of an open system in the behavioral school, and as we mentioned previously, the complexity of the problems facing the decision-maker, and the large number of internal, environmental, objective, and subjective factors that can affect the decision, made the decision-maker unable to link these variables and factors with each other, and then the rational and ideal decision-making.

As this comes as a result of the absence of concepts and the means at that time enable the decision-maker to be able to look at things holistically, as the various forms of functional approach remained trapped in the partial view of things, which made him incapable of providing a ground that satisfies getting correct and ideal decision-making.

Decision making hypotheses according to the behavioral approach

Through the behavioral approach, we can enumerate some of the assumptions that the management made when making the decision, based on the behavioral approach, including:

• Approaching realism when setting goals if the decision-maker fails to find the optimal alternative that achieves the goals at their maximum level, or in other words, in this case, he resorts to reducing the level of achieving the goals.

• Focuses the attention of the decision-makers in terms of priority on the first alternative that works to achieve the objective goals or solve the problems at hand.

• Since the decision-maker at that time did not possess the complete knowledge, the necessary information, and sufficient time to study the alternatives and to know their advantages and disadvantages in detail, this may have caused him to have limitations when studying the alternatives.

• One of the advantages that can be recorded for the decision-maker through the behavioral school is taking into account the cooperation between the members of the organization as well as the interaction between the conditions and factors of the internal and external environment affecting decision-making.

• The decision-maker's possession of the general idea of the problems and objectives, and his failure to arrange them according to their importance due to their multiplicity, in addition to that the arrangement criterion changes with the change of circumstances, which caused him to suffer the disadvantages of chaos arising from not arranging those alternatives and objectives.

Decision making steps according to the behavioral approach

The behavioral approach school views decision-making as rational and objective behavior, and it is made through four stages:

1- The diagnostic stage, which is the stage that includes forming an idea of the decision-making environment and the various cases in which this decision will be used.

2- *The design stage*, which is the stage through which known alternatives are identified and an appropriate analysis is conducted for the results of each alternative.

3- *The selection stage*, which is the stage in which the decision-maker selects the satisfactory alternative from a group of alternatives.

4- *The implementation stage*, which is the stage that includes designing specific programs to implement the chosen alternative.

Evaluation of the decision according to the behavioral approach

The behavioral school intended to describe the organization as a community member that performs integrated functions through a series of administrative decisions, and that member is associated with other members.

Organizations and other institutions with organizational relationships that together lead to the formation of the general social system. It also views the organization, institution, or company as an open system for dynamic decision-making within a general framework that has specific goals and alternatives.

Hence, the evaluation of the decision made by the organization, business enterprise, or related company must be based on the previous criteria to achieve their goals, and in a way that also achieves the goals of the society in which they are present.

Characteristics of the behavioral school and its disadvantages

This school distinguished between different types of rationalism, such as personal rationalism and objective rationalism, and the behaviorist school considered that organizations, institutions, and companies are like open system, it is affected by external and internal environmental factors.

This school also discovered shortcomings between the concept of objective rationalism and the economic criterion when making a decision, and between the decision-maker himself who cannot reach the optimal or appropriate solutions to the problem or crisis because the optimal or most appropriate alternative currently available may not be available tomorrow.

Also, among the obstacles that must be mentioned is the decision-maker's confrontation with many internal and external factors that he cannot control, and the alternative solutions available to the decision-maker may not be clear or known, and therefore the choice of one of these alternatives will prevent his ability and capabilities towards studying each of them and analyzing their results.

Chapter five ...
Hierarchical decision-making stages

The decision-making process generally goes through seven basic stages, which begin with diagnosing the problem or crisis and end with implementation and follow-up of the decision.

The stage of diagnosing the situation, problem, or crisis

The definition of a problem or crisis indicates that it is a state of deviation or imbalance that afflicts any system that works in its natural form, or a state that represents a desire for change or development, and therefore the diagnosis is represented in the accurate identification of the situation, problem or crisis and knowing its dimensions and effects, as this is done through the search for the causes generating either the problem or the desire for change or development.

The diagnosis process is considered one of the most important stages of decision-making because it defines the situation, problem, or crisis accurately and correctly, such things must ultimately lead to saving effort, money, and time as well as reducing the number of alternatives chosen for the solution or managing the situation.

Therefore, the decision-maker must be keen to seek seriously to study the situation, problem, or crisis in an in-depth manner in order to lay his hands on its causes, the circumstances in which it arose, and the consequences of not resolving it, or the required change or development, and the desired results to be gained from that.

The decision-maker must also differentiate between the problem or crisis and the phenomenon and between the main reasons for the emergence of the problem or crisis and the secondary ones that help to escalate its effects.

Subsequent to a real, buried problem or crisis, the decision-maker must consider some supporting factors when diagnosing the problem or crisis, namely:

• Taking into account all the circumstances surrounding the required change or development, or the problem or crisis and the consequences thereof to successfully manage the matter of change, development, or crisis.

• Emphasis on the need to solve chronic and complex problems or crises that affect the system of the organization, institution, or company, to avoid its continuation and development to the worst in the future.

• Not resorting to an analogy or attributing the problem or crisis presented to a problem or crisis that is characterized by the same phenomena and symptoms that may have occurred previously, because each problem or crisis has its nature and characteristics that are unique to it, only some of the alternatives that have been put forward to treat this problem or previous crisis can be resorted to if the effectiveness of this alternative is proven to treat the current problem or crisis.

• Move away, as much as possible, from substituting the personal assessment and self-assessment of the decision-maker, instead of scientific research towards identifying each of the required changes or development, or the problem or crisis.

The stage of analyzing the situation, problem or crisis

During the problem or crisis analysis stage, five processes are carried out, which are the processes of classification, categorizing, determination of nature, determination of size, and determination of the extent of complexity, provided that these operations are carried out by resorting to the following mechanisms:

• Determine the necessary data and information and the sources for obtaining them.

• Resorting to the use of modern information collection methods and information processing programs, such as databases, information systems, modeling and simulation, reports, statistics...etc.

• Work on dividing the problem or crisis into its basic components, regardless of the degree of complexity that characterizes it.

• Work on classifying and categorizing the elements and characteristics of the problem or crisis that afflicts the organization, institution, or company. There are routine problems that reflect the absence of workers, the distribution of work activities, or the breakdown of production lines...etc., and there are non-routine problems, such as low productivity, declining expected profits, rising costs, competing with other players in the market, changing customer or consumer tastes.... etc.

The stage of determining the standard required for decision-making alternatives

Among the important things that the decision-maker must take into account is to think carefully about the standard that will help him to choose between the alternatives presented to him to solve the problem or manage the crisis successfully, as these standards become the balance by which he weighs his solutions and compares between them, which is a quantitative or qualitative indicator that reflects an aspect of the problem and is of particular importance and works to bring the decision-maker closer to reach the general and basic goal of decision-making.

It should be noted that the standards always differ according to administrative situations and cases, and they also differ in terms of depth, comprehensiveness, quality, and composition.

Standards in terms of quality

• *Quantitative standards*, which are quantifiable, or that can be expressed in numbers with statistical, mathematical, natural, social, or economic significance, such as measures of central tendency, measures of dispersion and deviation, correlation and regression coefficients, mathematical functions, indices, and indicators that reflect quantitative aspects, for cases such as profits, costs, number of workers, lengths, weights, values, prices, sizes, and others.

• *Qualitative standards*, which are the standards that express the subjective state of the problem or crisis, and do not accept quantitative measurement, or it is impossible to measure quantitatively, such as pessimism, optimism, intelligence, and everything related to the moral aspects of the decision.

Standards in terms of impact (change over time)

• *Static standards (constant)*, are those standards whose value does not change with the change of time, but rather remains constant, such as temperature and blood pressure in living bodies under normal conditions, or indicators of mass attraction on the surface of the earth (gravity) and others, and here it must be noted that such standards we rarely find it in economic and social life because projects, organizations, business institutions, and companies are characterized by the movement and interaction.

• *Dynamic standards (movable)*, which are those standards whose value changes with the change of time, whether they are quantitative standards or qualitative standards, and are considered the most common in the world of management, economics, and sociology, such as moral values, tastes, economic returns, degrees of material satisfaction, calculating profits, costs and others.

Finally, it is worth pointing out that the decision-maker in organizations, institutions, or companies can use any kind of standards in any situation, or any occasion, based on the goal he wants to reach, and he must take into account that standards can carry multiple characteristics at the same time, for example, they are quantitative, complex and dynamic standards at the same time.

The situation of decision-making cannot be complex and simple at the same time, hence the thing to be imposed on the decision-maker is the type of standard that he will adopt towards evaluating the alternatives leading to the development or solving the problem or crisis and embodying his goal to be reached.

The stage of identifying and assembling alternatives

Of course, as we mentioned previously, each situation, each problem, and each crisis have its characteristics, even if they are similar to previous ones. Therefore, there may be some alternatives to this previous problem or crisis, not all of which may be suitable for addressing the situation under discussion, or the problem, or the ego crisis that can be resorted to.

Therefore, the decision-maker must be aware of that, and given that the problem or crisis does not arise from a vacuum, but rather it has multiple causes and effects that affect more than one side of the organization, institution, or company, the problem or crisis has many and multiple solutions, which are taken as alternatives to reach the desired solution, therefore, this stage is concerned with collecting and listing these alternatives according to the available information and data, but at the same time each alternative must meet the following conditions:

• That each alternative be assessable.

• That each alternative be available within the limits of available resources and capabilities.

• That each alternative can solve the problem or crisis or limit its effects.

The stage of conducting the evaluation of the available alternatives and the considerations of comparison between them

It is the stage through which the comparison process takes place between the alternatives offered to solve the problem or manage the crisis, through which the advantages and disadvantages of each of the alternatives are identified, and the extent to which each alternative contributes to the desired solution, and this stage is considered one of the most difficult stages for the decision-maker, given because the study and evaluation of alternatives are based on the expected results of using this alternative.

Those results do not appear except in the future. Accordingly, the decision-maker must take into account many considerations when choosing between alternatives as follows:

• Availability of appropriate conditions for the implementation of the chosen alternative.

• Calculating the costs of using the chosen alternative and its effects on the organization, institution, or company.

• Resorting to the use of all quantitative analysis methods to find out the expected results for each of the alternatives.

• Evaluation of all the differentiable alternatives according to specific criteria such as costs, suitability, identification with other factors in the organization, institution, or company...etc.

The stage of choosing the alternative, considerations, and criteria for decision-making

It is the stage through which one of the alternatives that are supposed to lead to the desired development, or solve the problem or crisis, or in the weakest faith, works to reduce the effects of this problem or crisis, is chosen, where the required choice is made in the light of many considerations, which includes economic, social, environmental, operational and legal considerations...etc., considering also the degree of knowledge and accuracy enjoyed by the decision-maker, the selection is made based on the accuracy of the information on which the choice (decision) is based, in addition to calculating the degree of risk and the capabilities and resources available to the organization, institution, or company.

The implementation phase of the alternative (implementation of the decision)

If we are in the process of implementing one of the decisions that have been made (one of the alternatives that have been chosen), then we must search for the nature and components of the environment in which the decision will be implemented and study it with knowing the surrounding circumstances until we reach the required results from the implementation of this decision.

The decision environment can be defined as the general climate in which the decision is taken, and it represents the qualitative and quantitative factors and influences that surround any center of a decision, and here we mean the organization, institution, or company, and that is what most distinguishes the conditions of this environment is interaction or dynamism and instability together, these matters must prompt the decision-maker when making (choosing the alternative) to identify each of the conditions and circumstances of the decision-implementation environment.

A- The circumstances of the decision implementation environment (alternative or solution)

The circumstances of the decision implementation environment have been summarized according to the following factors and influences:

1- Simple circumstances, which are the circumstances in which the factors and influences when implementing the decision are few and similar and remain unchanged in the decision centers, that is, in the organizations, institutions, or companies.

2- Complex circumstances, which are circumstances in which the factors and influences when implementing the decision are many and not similar, but remain unchanged in the decision-making centers.

3- Stable conditions, which are those conditions in which the factors and influences when implementing the decision are the same and unchanged.

4- Changing circumstances, which are circumstances in which factors and influences are highly variable and unpredictable.

The types of circumstances and the nature of cases related to the environment for implementing the decision

Nature of the circumstances	Simple	Complicated
Fixed	The factors and influences are few and the same *Routine-decision making* (Certain Status)	The factors and influences are many and not the same *Operational decision-making* (Risk Status)
Changing	The factors and influences are few and the same *Administrative decision-making* (Risk Status)	The factors and influences are many and not the same *Strategic decision-making* (Uncertain Status)

B - Cases of the decision implementation environment

Under this heading, we must point out that the multiplicity of environmental conditions under which the decision is implemented prompts the decision-maker to take into account many factors that may affect the process of implementing the decision, such as the degree of complexity toward implementation, and change, as well as the difference in the volume, type, and nature of available information that leads to distinguishing between three situations for decision-making, which are ***the state of certainty the state of uncertainty, and the state of risk***.

1- The state of certainty, is the state in which all of the information and data necessary for decision-making are available and known precisely, and there are no possibilities for any subjective or objective expected events, and therefore the decision-maker becomes fully and completely aware of the various alternatives he has and the results of each alternative. In other words, the decision-maker becomes fully aware of what may happen in the future and thus knows fully the types of variables that can occur, their behaviors, and their quantitative and qualitative effects on the situation, problem, or crisis, and the results of its solution in any of the paths that he will follow, and in this case, the decision maker will face two situations:

• Either the situation, the problem, or the crisis has a single and possible solution, such as defining some quantitative economic indicators, such as volumes, lengths, and weights, those that are governed by one of the available sources whose quantities are known accurately.

• Or the problem or crisis becomes has a limited number of alternative and possible solutions, as happens in the treatment of the problem of rationalization of plans to allocate available resources on possible and different aspects of use, and in this case, the decision-maker has to differentiate between the alternatives, and he must choose one of them from the group of possible alternatives, which achieves In the end, the goal of making this decision which based on a criterion or several quantitative or qualitative criteria.

Here we should point out that the decision-maker often encounters during the decision-making process, especially when listing the candidate alternatives to provide a solution, that the problem or crisis has many solutions that can be resorted to, the number of which may become unlimited.

In this case, the decision-maker must take the initiative to add new conditions and criteria that he may have neglected in the past, to codify the alternatives, limit them, and define them within a narrower scope to obtain a solution to the problem or crisis, otherwise, he will not be able in the end to make his decision, and he will drown its time in the details of the infinite alternatives.

2- *The state of Uncertainty*, a situation in which a sufficient amount of the required information and data is not available, constitutes a great difficulty for the decision-maker in estimating the possibilities for the different areas that are in contact with the problem or crisis.

To overcome this difficulty, the decision-maker will have to resort to relying on experience and preparing subjective probabilities that stem from him the nature of the results of each alternative, which is also the case in which the decision-maker may know the factors and variables that may occur in the future accurately, but he does not know and cannot predict the possibility of their occurrence.

In this case, the decision-maker must resort to his estimates, and this is what characterizes administrative decision-making with a subjective nature because it is ultimately related to the personal behavior of the decision-maker, his psychological state, and the extent of his optimism or pessimism about the future and its tendency to maximize the risk-return or reduce the loss by adopting a cautious stance.

3- *The case of risk*, is the case in which a certain amount of data and information is available about the alternatives and about the nature of the situation, problem, or crisis, but the results are linked to the expected possibilities of occurrence in the future, so the decision maker has to prepare a probability distribution that is based on objective evidence, and may be derived from other similar cases that occurred in the past, to estimate the results of each of the alternatives.

This case also assumes that the decision-maker fully knows the conditions and variables that can occur during the period that will be covered by the decision and that will affect the situation, problem, or crisis, but he does not know and cannot predict precisely what will happen, nor about the directions of change, the indicators of the decision during its implementation, rather, it may know the probability of what will happen, and the scope and possibilities of change, by forming a probabilistic distribution of expected events, which may result in the emergence of a double issue that the decision-maker must deal with, namely:

• Determine the conditions or variables that may occur in the future comprehensively and accurately.

• Determine the probability of occurrence of each of them.

And when talking about the possibilities to be determined by the decision maker, they will fall under three types, they are:

A - *Objective probabilities*, which are probabilities that are based on the laws of probabilities, especially the law of large numbers and the laws of probability distributions.

B- *Subjective probabilities*, which are the probabilities that are determined based on the decision-makers estimates, and perhaps with the support of his assistants from experts or advisors, which are those probabilities that depend on personal perception and self-faculties.

C- Conditional probabilities, which are the probabilities that are conditional on the occurrence of an event or a set of events, knowing the probability of its occurrence in advance and the degree of its impact on other variables related to the problem.

Standards of comparison between the cases that the organization is exposed to

Standard	Certain Status	Risk Status	Uncertain Status
Expected events	Generally known	Partially known	Completely unknown
Probabilities	100% Known	Probability of occurrence	100% unknown
Types of probabilities	Specific	Objective	Certainty is relative and risk available
Changing status	Stable - on one status	Specified and known in advance	Subjective
Results	Specific	Can be set	Can not be set

Chapter six …
Decision-Making out of the BOX

Today we need distinguished people who create events, formulate sustainable strategies, set goals that can be achieved, and manage difficult situations with their advanced tools, and all of this will only come by changing our view of things and going out of the crucible of indoctrination to the spaciousness of innovation.

Thinking out of the box is what is required from everyone today, and it is the basis and the effective solution to all management problems in its broad sense, and that is why we often hear about this term, and here some may ask about its meaning, and the meaning very simply refers to the person's exit from the box containing the issue, or the problem that he suffers and he has to stop his repeated attempts to solve it, also he has to face this situation as if he is not a party to this, for example, a person cannot assess the building's paint from the outside while he is inside that building, because in this case he simply has cannot see what is outside.

Thinking outside the box means your transformation from a routine person to an innovative person, and this will only come by re-educating yourself, accepting the idea of changing your thinking style, and learning some terms that will help you towards identifying what is meant by thinking outside the box, such as reformulating topics or solutions until you reach the optimal or most appropriate alternative, also try not to rely on one way of thinking, and learn what are the tools for self-development and the others for business development.

People with creative thinking outside the box are characterized by the ability to formulate creative and distinctive ideas to manage various topics and provide innovative solutions to problems, and this can only be achieved by adopting a willingness to think through new horizons of a sustainable nature in life and work, that is, adopting a method of thinking in different ways and with a mind open about what was prevalent, focus on the essence of the presented topics, or problems, and can accept different reactions, work to develop new ideas and ways to work on them, identify the value obtained from them, can listen, care, respect and support the creative ideas of others, and strive always working in a team spirit, we are always reminding that the vision of eight eyes is better than six eyes, better than four eyes, and certainly better than two eyes.

For you to make your decision outside the box to be adequate and complete, you must change your way of thinking that you are used to or develop it by what you want to reach, and this will only come by merging logic with innovation to obtain creativity and this is what many types of research that have been conducted refer to this matter.

The integration of logic with innovation to reach creativity must require the availability of some tools, means, and the self-preparation of the individual in order to achieve this result. Among these tools and means is to change our thinking style from what is scientifically called linear thinking, or stereotypical thinking, to adopting a non-linear thinking style, or innovative thinking.

Linear or stereotypical thinking acquired its definition from the path it takes, which comes in the form of a continuous line through which ideas are sent, or what we can call the stations of the thinking way for a specific topic, which comes in the form of consecutive shapes in order and sequential to complete the idea, and as shown in this illustrator.

Linear style of thinking

Cause ... "affecting"   *Event ... "effected"*

Variable (A) ⟶ (B) **Variable**

Most of us think linearly...   *Many of us think logically...*

cause   cause   cause   cause   cause   cause

(A) (B) (C) (D) (E) (?) ......

effect   effect   effect   effect   effect

The effects of variables in the linear path takes one interactive direction

According to this style of thinking, the outcome of the subject under discussion by resorting to this method for decision-making will eventually refer to the expected result, which will often reflect a purely logical return, i.e., an alternative or a solution that may carry the remedy for some issues, and may fail to treat some other issues, this is the dilemma of pure logic that is suitable for example in concluding clear and logical contracts to preserve the interests of the parties.

Pure logic is not suitable for some paths of settling disputes between adversaries that are characterized by special natures, and therefore the decision-maker must turn to another mode of thinking in order to bridge this gap that arises from resorting to pure logic, this can be achieved by moving towards the innovative way of thinking that is reflected in the non-linear method as shown in this illustration.

Non-linear style of thinking

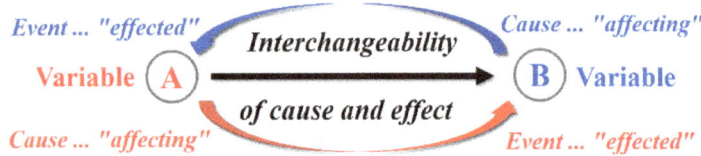

Some of us think linearly...   Few of us think creatively...

*The effects of the variables in the non-linear
path take a reciprocal looping direction*

The pattern of nonlinearity in thinking comes in the form of a loop that connects two variables (two stations of thinking), one of which is called the cause (i.e., the reason for the birth of an event), and the second is called the event (i.e., the effect arising from this cause), and from that what is called feedback is generated from the interacting relationship between this cause and the event, through which the path of thinking required to handle a subject is determined, or to make a related decision.

This style of thinking is characterized by discovering side effects on the course of thinking that may not be monitored by following a purely logical thinking style, and thus the decision-maker becomes fully aware of what the decision can achieve when implemented.

Integrating both the logical and the innovative side of what is involved in the topic related to decision-making will result in creative results for this decision.

Among the other effective methods that the decision-maker must resort to is the brainstorming process that must take place with the seekers of this decision-making.

Where brainstorming is also considered a method for developing the skills of the decision-maker and contributing to a creative solution to problems and complexities by addressing what we can call the hidden or imperceptible matters of the decision-maker, as well as the unknown assumptions, or unrealistic, or restrictions that may cause the decision-maker to stumble because he is not aware of them.

This is one of the reasons why making effective thinking needed by the decision-maker to interact with others to discover and identify these constraints and manage them properly.

Among the other methods that the decision-maker can resort to get out of the crucible of the thinking box in which he lived for long periods to the wide range of different areas of thinking outside this box, is what the well-known thinker and writer **Edward de Bono** exposed in his training program entitled **The Five-Day Course in Thinking in**, presented in 1968, during which he made a comparison between the vertical thinking that the public generally resorts to, and what is called lateral thinking (side thinking) that raises the research faculty of the thinker and makes him give up the gradual approach of the thinking path, instead of the vertical thinking method that takes a single direction.

From the following illustration, we can discover the minutes of comparisons between these two types of thinking methods, as indicated by de Bono.

Vertical thinking	Lateral thinking
Chooses	Changes
Looks for what is right	Looks for what is different
One thing must follow from another	Makes deliberate jumps directly
Concentrates on relevance	Welcomes chance intrusions
Moves in the most likely directions	Explores the least likely directions

Lateral thinking (side thinking) often leads to the opposite of what appears to be the natural or logical way of doing things. For example, in the beginnings of car manufacturing operations, workers in factories would make one car with all its components at a time, and then move on to manufacture another one, and so on in a sequential manner, while today the assembly lines of car components in factories have become the master of the situation.

This correct decision resulted in a good distribution of work, and an increase in the issue of specializations among workers, some of whom are keen on assembling the engine, and the others whose responsibility is to install the engine inside the body of the car, the third is specialized in lighting, the fourth is in the installation of doors, and so on. Here, we have to refer to Henry Ford, the decision-maker for establishing car assembly lines.

It is important to think sideways (laterally), because the seeds of solving a problem or managing a specific topic that requires decision-making may lie outside the framework of this problem or topic, which requires the creative decision-maker to activate the skill of searching for these seeds to identify and manage them and its effects as required, and this need resorting to the methodology of division and fragmentation of relevant information to reach the basis of these seeds.

Creative decision-makers must always be ready to challenge widely accepted assumptions because thinking outside the box means the ability to identify the assumptions, habits, or traditional ways of thinking that are widely accepted and uncritical but have no basis in reality.

Training on the issue of expanding the perceptions of thinking by the decision-maker will provide him with additional possibilities to purify the details of the decision to be made from any impurities or deficiencies, the decision-maker stands helpless in front of him, as it is not possible to force the creative thinking of his mind to be effective throughout the twenty-four hours. That is why it would be better, in this case, to leave the issue of making decision vocabulary for a while and allow the subconscious mind, (the deep mind of the decision maker), to take the initiative until the expected answer comes suddenly.

Understanding the principle of the depth of mind can open the way for the decision-maker to adopt a more creative approach towards solving problems, or managing issues at hand, while many people are still not even aware that their deep minds can perform important mental functions for them, such as gathering parts into new groups, or create new connections as they are engaged in other activities, and we have to be convinced that possible solutions and courses of action almost immediately begin to appear in front of us when there is some kind of time delay, it means that the deeper parts of the brain have been called to work and provided what can contribute to it.

Vocabulary for creative thinking

For the decision-maker to become a creative thinker, this matter will require him to be trained to follow a certain methodology or specific steps to reach his goal of deciding on the box, *these steps begin with good preparation for the issue of the decision, followed by the stage of briefing this issue from all its aspects, then the stage of careful examination of the subject, and finally the stage of evaluating the solution (the decision) and its conformity with the correct implementation.*

1- The preparation stage, which is the stage that includes hard work, collecting relevant information, sorting and classifying it, analyzing the problem or topic as accurately as possible, and exploring in principle possible solutions.

2- The incubation stage is the stage that is specific to deep thinking, which includes analysis, synthesis, and assessment of the problem or topic under discussion, and it is the stage in which the subconscious mind plays an important role because it is exposed to dealing with the matter as separate parts, and the formation of new components, which may include other ones stored away in the memory of the decision-maker.

3- The stage of foresight, which is the stage that the decision-maker experiences while he is in a comfortable state of mind, where a new idea may appear in his conscious mind, either gradually or suddenly, and these moments often occur when the decision-maker is far from the problem or the main topic under discussion in his thinking.

4- *The validation stage* is the stage through which the decision-makers self-capacity is activated towards adopting the opinion reached, and it includes testing the new idea, insight, intuition, expectation, or solution accurately, to confirm that what has been reached is a correct decision which will form the basis for the required action.

Mental barriers

Also, among the factors that the decision-maker must take into account are the so-called mental barriers that can limit the effectiveness of his work, including ***lack of facts, disbelief, lack of a starting point, lack of perspective on the problem or topic under discussion, and lack of motivation***.

1- *Lack of facts*: when the decision-maker is not sure that he has all the facts related to the problem or topic, in this case, it is natural for him to hesitate to commit to doing more research, and this may make him move again in other directions to complete these facts.

2- *Disbelief*: the decision-maker may find it difficult to believe the matter, due to the lack of conviction of the value of the subject under discussion.

3- *Lack of a starting point*: the problem or topic under discussion may seem so big that the decision-maker does not know where to start, which leaves him free to choose to start from the place closest to his perception, with the possibility of changing this place at a later time if necessary, with knowing that inspiration will come to the decision-maker after it has begun, not before.

4- *Lack of perspective*: the decision-maker may be very close to the problem or topic under discussion, especially if he has lived with it for a long time, or has always been concerned about it. Consulting others who are close to this matter, asking for help to direct the vision to new angles that work to change the perspective.

5- *Lack of motivation*: it is known that creative thinking requires perseverance in the face of difficulties that can be overcome, and therefore the decision-maker's lack of motivation towards that may push him to postpone researching the matter entrusted to him to overcome this feeling, and then reactivate his feeling towards achieving the goal that he seeks through his work related to the relevant decision-making.

Undoubtedly, the importance of creative thinking towards solving problems and managing complex issues is confirmed through the creation of new ideas, and this will not happen in isolation from resorting to the use of evaluation skills of the decision-maker, those skills that in part must find an answer to such questions:

*- Is this issue recent / Is this topic new?

*- This problem or topic will involve who?

*- Will resorting to making this decision require a more formal evaluation?

*- Are the solutions that can be reached considered appropriate and practical?

*- What is the amount of savings that can be obtained from making this decision?

*- How much will the decision-making cost to solve this problem or manage this issue?

In this interactive era, we live, which is characterized by rapid change, the decision-maker, in addition to his skills as a creative thinker, must have productive and constructive thinking, and the decision-maker must possess the skill of analysis and logical vision, which gives him a third dimension when making decisions and solving problems.

Chapter seven ...
Developing thinking skills of the decision maker

The development of creative thinking skills is not one of the academic subjects that are taught in universities and higher institutes, just as there is no official body related to knowledge supported by empirical research in connection with this matter. If the decision-maker wants to develop his thinking skills, then his task is basically, to focus on self-development.

How to become an effective and practical thinker and decision maker?

Forming a clear picture of the thinker you want to be as a decision-maker is the first step that you must take, and therefore a clear concept of what you want to become one day can be a point of attraction for you, always remember this point that relates to the formulation of the rank you want to become in it, and define the date of reaching it and then think back to what you are now to feel the difference.

As a decision maker, you can do this by talking to yourself through abstract phrases, mentioning all the qualities, knowledge, jobs, or skills that you want to acquire by the date that you have previously determined, and working to record this in the form of a categorized list that includes all these topics, provided that you begin to choose between all qualities, knowledge, jobs, and skills until you reach what you feel is easy to acquire, and is appropriate to your thinking.

The decision-maker can identify some of the distinguished thinkers who admire him and whom he tends to appreciate, to identify their historical path made them reach the distinction they have now, through knowing them personally or studying them deeply by reading more than one of their biographies for example, identifying the thinking skills that impress the concerned decision-maker.

Among the means that make you an effective and practical thinker to make the right decisions, is to take someone who possesses creative thinking skills as your mentor, and this mentor must have the skills of analysis, synthesis, evaluation, decision-making, problem-solving, and creative thinking. This mentor may be someone closest to you, such as a parent, friend, life partner, or manager you worked for at some time.

Now, as a decision-maker, you can begin to form a composite and imaginative image of yourself as an ideal and effective thinker, who possesses analytical skills, rich and creative imagination, enjoys flexibility and improvisation, issues exceptional judgments in situations of uncertainty or unpredictability, and dares to manage calculated risks, and the availability of intuitive sense about what is happening behind the scenes, and far from arrogance and he is openness towards criticism and has a spirit of decisiveness when asking for decision-making, and bears ambiguity when it is not time to make a decision.

The right decision maker in the right place

It should be noted that thinking skills are organically linked to the issue of decision-making and problem-solving because it is radically linked to a specific field and has a close relationship with knowledge, traditions, customs, and values, and therefore it would be better to choose people who have the motivation to develop their thinking skills, as it is very difficult to learn abnormal skills that are difficult for the decision-maker, and therefore it will always be better for him to choose the appropriate field for him as a thinker so that he can make his decisions correctly.

Therefore, he should answer some questions that may help him towards choosing the field in which he will excel:

A- What are your interests?

Interests are a state of feeling that the decision-maker wishes to pay special attention to and that long-term interests are important and drive towards acquiring the required knowledge and skills.

B- What are your abilities?

Abilities are skills that reflect competence and the ability to learn or acquire a specific skill.

C- The nature of the personality?

The nature of their personality reflects the general and prevailing mood of him. Some, for example, become uncomfortable in decision-making situations that are full of pressures, or that are characterized by risks, and others bear the stressful nature of this type of decision.

In addition to the above, it will be easier for the decision-maker to identify the areas that suit him, away from those that lack the necessary level of interest, mental competence, or temperamental characteristics to do them well.

Vocabulary of a self-learning strategy to prepare the decision maker

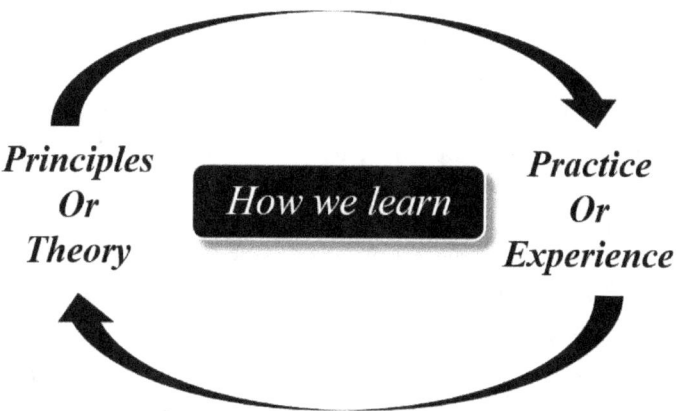

Principles Or Theory — *How we learn* — **Practice Or Experience**

It will be of great importance, before the decision-maker plans his self-learning program, to be aware of the basic rules on which he will be based to achieve this, and as the above illustration indicates, that is, to rely on each of the principles or theories, and on practice or experience, and not to lose sight of the trends that this was achieved, in the sense that the decision-maker relies on the relevant principles and then turns to practice, as well as relying on experience to confirm what was stated in the relevant theories.

Since decision-making and problem-solving are among the central activities in human life, which leads to the creation of a scope that expands daily, and related to the accumulation of self-experience, learning from mistakes, mastering the technical aspects of business, and acquiring knowledge related to principles or theories, which are matters that have a great impact on people's practices and life, this will undoubtedly push the decision-maker to work towards applying some learning methods to develop his thinking skills through some practical proposals included in the following context:

• Getting used to reading books related to your work as a decision-maker, and that this reading is characterized by focusing and reflection, extracting all the basic principles covered by each book, and identifying models or frameworks that you can use so that you can finally form what we can call your theoretical group related to your practices.

• Complementary to what is mentioned above, set yourself a specific program for reading books, and try to keep reading books related to leadership in general, to get to know the features and nature of this leadership. Examine the biography of a prominent leader in your field of work in the organization, and then write down the basic principles that this leader enjoys, to add these principles to your previously mentioned theoretical group.

• Transfer the growing collection of principles, examples, practical tips, sayings or quotes, and mini case studies into your notebook containing what we called your theoretical set, keep reading it backward, and relate it to your current experience.

• It will be useful for you to make an inventory of your thinking skills related to your field of work from time to time, to identify your strengths, as well as weaknesses that need to be improved and strengthened.

• As we mentioned previously, the directive (mentor) for you to develop your thinking skills may be the closest to you. It would be useful to know if it was possible to identify three distinguished decision makers and problem solvers in your field whom you can reach and to apply for the possibility of an interview with them, even if briefly to discover the principles and ways in which they developed as applied thinkers.

• Choose one of the worst decisions that were adopted and implemented in your organization during the last period of a few months, and consider the terms and effects of this decision as a case study for you. Discover the lessons learned from the negative effects of implementing this decision by focusing on its weaknesses, such things will increase your confidence towards avoiding such negatives that your future decisions may include.

• Choose one of the distinguished innovations in your field within the organization in which you work, knowing that the word innovation refers to a new idea that has been successfully launched in the market as a new or renewable product or service.

Consider the vocabulary of this decision related to this innovation and its impact as a case study for you. Discover the positive effects of applying this decision by calculating its strengths, such things will increase your knowledge about the positives that your future decisions may include, and that will contribute to the creative treatment and solving problems.• Take advantage of any opportunity that comes to you in order to attend courses or seminars that provide you with technical know-how in the general field of effective thinking, which will always make you fully aware of what information technology can do for business management and problem-solving.

• Finally, as a decision-maker, you must do your best to search for criticism directed at you as a decision-maker and problem solver, with the knowledge that severe criticism of yourself from others, no matter how negative it may seem, you still need it in order to learn, which is the hardest part towards being a self-educator, and you must admit that your critics, whatever their motives or morals, are doing you a great help as if they were your close friends.

This is the vocabulary of the strategy and the components of your program for self-learning as a creative decision-maker out of the box. In any self-learning program, experience plays a major role in it, and as a result, the reward will be represented in developing both your knowledge of process, skills and your ability to apply that knowledge in all difficult situations that arise you may be exposed to it.

Chapter eight …
Discipline and rationality in organizations

Mini workshop

Decision making for business development

Through this mini-workshop, we will discover the scenario that the decision-maker can adopt to formulate a decision in the correct and required manner, as this example indicates the tendency of a company towards decision-making, which ultimately leads to the rationalization of expenses.

Rationalizing the administrative expenses of Al-Ghad Real Estate

Scenario the decision-making and implementation

Of course, this scenario will start with **the stage of diagnosing the situation**, to identify the desired goal of making this decision, which is of course rationalizing the company's expenses, measuring the importance of this decision on the financial resources of this company, and the results of that decision on the company's performance, and exploring the effects of this decision on the short and long-term.

Following this the decision-maker resorts to **the stage of defining the required criteria**, which are the criteria for the research methodology related to the subject of the decision, and the relevant work tracks.

Then going to **the case analysis stage**, which is the stage related to the details of the tracks that will be worked on to reach the required rationalization, which will be, for example, the track of costs in general, the track of purchase prices of raw materials, the track of employment, the track of suppliers...etc.

Upon completion of the study of the vocabulary of the case analysis stage, the move is made to **the stage of identifying the alternatives or solutions**, that is, knowing the alternatives for each of those tracks and compiling them in a specific list or table.

The next stage is **the evaluation stage of the alternatives** that were compiled in the form of a table to limit the evaluation process.

After the completion of this stage, **the stage of selection of the alternative or solution** is taken, through the process of comparison between the alternatives, followed by the selection of the most appropriate or optimal alternative, and the last stage is ***the stage of implementing the decision***, with determining the time limit and recommendations for implementation.

References

*- Alder, H (1995) Think like a Leader: 150 top business leaders show you how their minds work, Piatkus, London.

*- de Bono, E (1968) The Five-Day Course in Thinking, McGraw-Hill, Maidenhead.

*- de Bono, E (1971) Lateral Thinking for Management, McGraw-Hill, Maidenhead

*- de Bono, E (1971) The Use of Lateral Thinking, Penguin, London.

*- de Bono, E (1985) Six Thinking Hats, Penguin, London.

*- Buzan, T (1974) Use Your Head, BBC Publications, London.

*- Culligan, M J, Deakins, C S and Young, A H (1983) Back to Basics Management, Facts on File, New York.

*- Dawson, R (1994) Make the Right Decision Every Time, Nicholas Brealey, London.

*- Drucker, P (1966) The Effective Executive, Harper & Row, New York.

*- Drucker, P (1967) The Practice of Management, Heinemann, London.

*- Kepner, C H and Tregoe, B (1965) The Rational Manager, McGraw-Hill, London.

*- Koestler, A (1964) The Act of Creation, Hutchinson, London.

*- Rawlinson, J G (1983) Creative Thinking and Brainstorming, Gower, Aldershot.

*- Thompson, R (1975) After I Was Sixty, Hamish Hamilton, London.

www.ingramcontent.com/pod-product-compliance
Lightning Source LLC
Chambersburg PA
CBHW070317240526
45467CB00045B/551